GUIDANCE FOR TODAY

HOW TO BE LED BY GOD

ACKNOWLEDGEMENTS

Many of the insights found in this book have been drawn from the writings of Charles Swindol, Joyce Meyer and T.D. Jakes. I highly recommend their materials.

GUIDANCE FOR TODAY

HOW TO BE LED BY GOD

BOB GASS

SYNERGY PUBLISHERS
Gainesville, Florida 32635

All scriptures are taken from the King James Version unless otherwise noted.

Other Bible Translations used as noted:

TM	- The Message
NIV	- New International Version
NLT	- New Living Translation
LB	- Living Bible
AMP	- Amplified Bible
NKJV	- New King James Version
NCV	- New Century Version

GUIDANCE FOR TODAY: HOW TO BE LED BY GOD
ISBN 1-931727-02-P
Copyright ©2001 by Bob Gass
Library of Congress Catalog Card Number: Pending

SYNERGY PUBLISHERS
Gainesville, Florida 32635

Printed in the United States of America. All rights reserved.
Under International Copyright Law, no part of this publication may be reproduced, stored, or transmitted by any means—electronic, mechanical, photographic (photocopy), recording, or otherwise— without written permission from the Publisher.

TABLE OF CONTENTS

PREFACE

In this book, you'll find practical, down-to-earth insights on ... recognizing God's voice ... knowing His timing ... learning His methods ... and understanding His plan for your life.

You have the *right* to expect His guidance. You also have the *responsibility* to consult Him on everything you do. Listen, "In all thy ways acknowledge him, and he shall direct thy paths" (Pr 3:6).

This is a workbook. Keep it handy - its principles are timeless. When you're not sure what to do or which way to go, God's promise to you is, "Along *unfamiliar paths* I will guide them; I will turn the darkness into light before them and make the rough places smooth. These are the things I will do; I will not forsake them" (Isa 42:16 NIV).

Listen again, "He calls his own sheep by name

and leads them out. He walks ahead of them …
for they recognize his voice" (John 10:3-4 LB).

Guidance: God's promised it to you - that's
what this book is all about.

1

IT'S ALL INCLUDED

Did you hear about the man who bought a ticket on a cruise ship and took with him a supply of cheese and crackers?

Every day at mealtime he retreated to his room and sat eating his rations. Toward the end of the cruise, the Captain asked him if he was unhappy with the food service. "No, it looks wonderful," he replied. The Captain asked, "Then why haven't we seen you in the dining room? I understand you've been sitting in your cabin eating cheese and crackers." The man responded, "That's because when I paid for my ticket, I didn't have anything left for meals." To his embarrassment and dismay the Captain replied, *"The price of the meals was included in your ticket!"*

Think; he could have been enjoying breakfast, lunch, high-tea, dinner, and a late-night banquet on the promenade deck! Instead he settled for cheese and crackers in his cabin, all because he didn't *know* what was available to him or how to take advantage of it.

Peter says, "Everything that goes into a life of pleasing God has been miraculously given to us" (2Pe 1:3 TM). Did you hear that? Everything! *That includes - guidance.*

God told Abraham when to leave home (Ge 12:1) and Jacob when to go back (Ge 31:3). When David asked Him if he should go to battle, He said, "Go, for I will surely hand the Philistines over to you" (2Sa 5:19 NIV). He even told Elijah where to find food in the middle of famine (1Ki 17:1-5), and His promise to you is, "Along unfamiliar paths I will guide them ..." (Isa 42:16 NIV). The path you're on today may be unfamiliar to you, but it's not to God. All you need is a *desire* to be led, and the *faith* to step out and follow Him.

God never changes. If He talked to people all through the Bible, He'll talk to you too. The question is, have you learned to recognize His voice yet?

Nothing should be more important to you than learning to hear from God for yourself. The ideas of others should only confirm or clarify what He has *already* told you. If you haven't first heard from Him, you'll be tempted to think that their ideas are His commands. That could be fatal.

You are unique! God has a personal plan and a specific destination for you. Take the time to ask Him about it for His Word says, "He guides the humble in what is right and teaches them his way" (Ps 25:9 NIV).

All you need to begin, is a little humility.

2

SERENDIPITY -
THE GOD OF SURPRISES

Do you remember the story of *The Three Princes of Serendipity*? It's about three rulers who set out to find treasure, but while they are looking for it, they find something much better. From this story we get the wonderful word *"serendipity."* It means to live expecting surprises - and God has lots of them for you!

He surprised a shepherd called Moses, by speaking to him from a burning bush, saying, "I'm sending you to Pharaoh to say, 'Let my people go'" (Ex 5:1). And how about Paul? As one door after another slams shut without explanation, he's suddenly surprised by a man from Macedonia calling to him in a vision, "Come over here and help us" (Acts 16:9 LB). The result? The non-Jewish world hears the Gospel for the first time. If you're a

Gentile, that's worth celebrating!

All through history God keeps showing up unexpectedly and changing things. And He's still the God of surprises, who says to you, "See, I am doing a new thing! Now it springs up: do you not · perceive it?" (Isa 43:19 NIV). Ah, there's the challenge - our perception. Either we fail to recognize His voice, or to trust that it's really *Him* speaking to us.

Maybe you're saying, "If you knew my situation, you'd understand that nothing is ever going to change." Don't say that. You're contradicting God! The Bible says, "Therefore will the Lord wait, that he may be gracious unto you" (Isa 30:18). Did you hear that? He's just *waiting* to show you what He can do for you, if only you'll talk to Him and take the time to listen!

Solomon says, "Many are the plans in a man's heart, but it is the Lord's purpose that prevails" (Pr 19:21 NIV). Even though your plans are imperfect, if your heart is right, God will *still* make things turn out for your good and His glory.

Are you having difficulty sorting out your ideas from His? We all struggle with that, especially when the Bible doesn't give us specifics. For example, when it's time to move, or marry, or change jobs, what do you do? God says, "I will instruct thee and teach thee in the way which thou shalt go" (Ps 32:8). You say, "That's nice, but I'd like a little more detail. How can I know it's God and not me?" Here are three things I've learned about God's guidance over the years:

First, ideas go away, but His direction stays. There's persistence in His leading; that's why time is on your side.

Second, His direction is usually impossible to follow without Him. He plans it that way. Jesus said, "Without me you can do nothing" (Jn 15:5). Paul confessed, "The less I have, the more I depend on him" (2Co 12:10 LB). This is what I call "forced dependence," and the independent streak in all of us hates it.

Third, His direction usually begins with discomfort. Listen, "Like an eagle stirs up its nest … the Lord alone led him" (Dt 32:11-12 NIV). A young eagle only learns to fly when its mother pushes it out of the nest and over the cliff's edge. Can you imagine its thoughts? "It's my *mother* doing this to me!" Yet only when it's forced out of its comfort zone, does the eagle discover its wings, release its power, and find its place in the sky.

Has God been stirring up your nest?

3

HEARING THE VOICE OF GOD

Hearing from God changes everything! But I've discovered that there are seven particular occasions when it makes *all* the difference.

1. Hearing from Him before you consider the needs of others. Why? Because *their* needs are driving them; only the plan of God should be leading you.

2. Hearing from Him before you entertain the ideas of others. Why? Because their ideas are not His commands. Be careful; it's easier to get into things than it is to get out of them. Don't make wrong commitments and end up bound by promises you can't fulfill. Love others, but be led only by God's Spirit.

3. Hearing from Him before you listen to the complaints of others. Why? Because you are not responsible for their happiness. Stop being so co-dependent - needing to fix them in order to feel good about yourself! Turn them over to God and get back into focus.

4. Hearing from Him before you make any significant changes. Why? Because it's not your job to *decide* what God wants you to do; it's your job to *discover* it.

5. Hearing from Him before you respond to the requests of others. Why? Because only then will you be able to discern what's behind their requests. *Qualify the soil before you sow.* Your seed is too precious to waste.

6. Hearing from Him before you share your dreams with others. Why? Because certain people will scorn them or even try to sabotage them. Remember Joseph's brothers? When Satan wants to discourage you, he'll use a person; often one who's not even aware of the spirit that's at work within him. Listen, "[He] rebuked them, and said Ye know not what ... spirit ye are of" (Lk 9:55). Think; Jesus was speaking to *His own disciples* here.

7. Hearing from Him before you seek the approval of others. Why? Because people with their own agendas will use flattery to manipulate you. Hearing God's voice, however, will keep you from falling into their trap.

The bottom line is this; pray, submit yourself to God, and then ask for His direction before you make any important decision.

4

WALKING WITH GOD

It would be impossible to count the number of books on the market today telling you how to set your own goals and achieve them.

Now while these books may be helpful, you need to understand that God is not committed to *anything* other than His foreordained plan for your life. You can't come to Him and say, "Here's my idea, please stamp Your approval on it." That's not the way it works. Listen, "He has created us ... so that we can do the good things he planned for us long ago" (Eph 2:10 NLT). Your prayer must be, "Lord, show me *Your* plan!"

You can't compartmentalize your life by saying, "In *this* category I'm doing things my way, but in *that* category I'm being led by God." No, *every* step you take must be synchronized with the beat of the Holy Spirit. Once you understand that, nothing will be more important to you than keeping pace with Him.

Paul writes, "For it is God who works *in you* to will and to act according to his good purpose" (Php 2:13 NIV). God works *through* us as we engage our minds, open our mouths, move our feet, and use our hands to do what He has *already* put into our hearts.

The moment you say "Yes" to Him, He gives you the ability to perform His will. Notice He doesn't reveal His will to you first then call you next. No, He calls you, and, as you step out to obey Him, He reveals it to you step by step and empowers you to carry it out.

God is never content with the status quo! Every day in countless ways He'll mold and develop you into a greater likeness of His Son. You're not out for a stroll, you're going somewhere! Over and over again you'll be given experiences and put into situations that'll mature you to the point where you have the same attitude, the same perspective, and the same discernment as Jesus.

When you begin to understand that, walking with God will take on a whole new meaning. You'll realize that your walk with Him is the *only* walk that will ever satisfy you or fulfill your purpose for being on this earth.

5

In Harmony

Paul writes, "According as he hath chosen us in him" (Eph 1:4). One of the keys to understanding God's will for your life is found in the word *"according."* It's a musical term that means, "in harmony with."

Now, to be in harmony with someone, you've got to understand that: (a) the melody always takes the lead; (b) the harmony must have an ear to hear and a willingness to follow; (c) it takes time and practice to get it right; (d) an instrument can be thrown off key through lack of use or poor maintenance.

Are you getting the idea? Your job is to recognize God's purpose for your life and choose *only* those things that harmonize with it. The question is not merely, "Is it right or wrong?" The question should be, "Is it right for *me*?"

One of life's greatest experiences is to be wanted and chosen by another person. It's the supreme antidote to loneliness, depression, and low self-esteem. But as wonderful as it is, it pales in comparison to being wanted and chosen by God. Imagine; God has chosen you to walk and live in harmony with Him. Awesome!

This means that *how you process information and arrive at conclusions* must always be subjected to His will. Paul describes the process this way: "Put off your old self … [and] put on the new self" (Eph 4:22-23 NIV).

Now, when you first start thinking *God's* way, it'll feel strange to you. You might even think, "This is just a put on." But it's not. Just as new shoes don't immediately feel comfortable when you put them on, so your new way of approaching life won't feel comfortable to you either. But as you *continue* to put on "the new self," you become more and more comfortable with it.

It works like this. You have to: (a) *practice*

being nice, until you automatically become nice; (b) *practice* going to church on Sunday, until going anywhere else on Sunday seems strange to you; (c) *practice* giving to God until it becomes as natural to you as buying a new outfit at the mall; (d) *practice* telling the truth, until even the smallest lie turns sour in your mouth; (e) *practice* speaking kindness, until every cynical, negative word is purged from your vocabulary.

It's a matter of practice!

But, you ask, "Isn't that being hypocritical - feeling one way and speaking another?" No, it's just *retraining* yourself to walk God's way, and *restraining* yourself from walking any other way. You are literally declaring, "Lord, it's no longer a matter of anything goes in my life. From now on it's what *You* say and direct me to do."

6

BE CONFIDENT

Have you noticed how often *"they"* decide what's important for us and what's not? For example, *"they"* say the Chairman of the Board is important-but the cleaning lady is not. If you buy into that nonsense, you'll become inferior, insecure, resentful, and competitive. You'll also strive to become what *"they"* approve of - and in the process risk missing what God wants you to be.

Or worse, you'll actually *do* what God has called you to do, but never get any joy or fulfillment out of it, because *"they"* planted so much self-doubt in your mind. Refuse to live that way another day!

It takes courage to be led by God's Spirit. It's not easy to break the mold of family, or step outside the boundaries others have set for you. When you do, you'll face disapproval and even rejection.

Jesus did. When *"they"* said, "Isn't this the carpenter's son?" (Mt 13:55 NIV), they were saying, "He should stay in His place." Look out, they'll say that about you too!

Paul says, "Each of us will give an account of himself to God" (Ro 14:12). In the final audit, you'll answer to God alone. In that moment, you'll discover that not only is it wrong to be judgmental, it's *equally wrong* to permit the opinions of others to control you, or cause you to miss God's will for your life.

Listen, "Blessed is the man who trusts in the Lord, whose confidence is in him" (Jer 17:7 NIV). To follow God's leading you must have confidence - not self-confidence - that (a) He loves you unconditionally; (b) He has a wonderful plan for your life; (c) you're capable of hearing from Him for yourself; (d) whatever He asks of you, He'll enable you to do.

A lot of our frustration comes from *misplaced* confidence. Listen, "Cursed is the one who ...

depends on flesh for his strength" (Jer 17:5 NIV). God will not allow you to succeed until you've learned to place your confidence in *Him* alone.

We all have a destiny. But just because we were born to do something, doesn't mean it'll automatically happen. I made a lot of mistakes while God was developing me. At one point I got so discouraged, I felt like getting out of the ministry. But even then, God was at work in my life. The Bible says that we go "from faith to faith" (Ro 1:17). In those days it seems like I went from faith to doubt, and then back to faith.

But gradually I learned (yes, you have to learn it, and it takes time), how to be confident in God, confident in my calling, and confident in my ability to be led by Him.

When you know you've heard from God, be resolute! Things worth having never come easy. If you find yourself weakening, ask God for determination! It's something that's in Him, and He *imparts* it to us through His Spirit. Therefore, we are not quitters, or the type of people who are easily defeated.

If you find yourself being "double-minded" about something, go back and ask yourself what God told you in the beginning - then stick with it! Don't go in a different direction because of worry, or discouragement, or the opinions of others.

Remind yourself constantly that you have what it takes to succeed in whatever God has called you to do! If you've accepted Jesus Christ as Lord of your life, His determination lives in you - because *He* lives in you.

But you must learn to be sensitive to His voice. When He speaks to you, it won't be like a hammer pounding on your head. No, it will be more like a gentle prompting inside you. Listen, "We serve ... [under obedience to the promptings] of the Spirit" (Ro 7:6 AMP).

Now you can ignore His promptings, disobey them, argue with them, or even try to postpone them. When you do that, however, you finish up under stress. When you disobey God, how could it be otherwise? (1Jn 3:21-22).

The word *obedience* is a turn-off to many of us. Right away we think of God asking us for a huge sum of money, sending us to the mission field, or telling us to do something we don't want to do.

Get real! If you won't listen to Him when He tells you to turn off your television and spend ten minutes with Him in prayer, what makes you think He'd tell you to go to the mission field?

Obeying God in *little* things, not big ones, is the key to learning how to be led by Him. For example, when He prompts you not to say another word but you keep right on talking - *that's* when you get into arguments and your stress levels go through the roof. Ever do that?

God's Word says, "If you will listen diligently to the voice of the Lord your God ... you shall be above only, and you shall not be beneath" (Dt 28:1 & 13 AMP). The difference between being *under* the situation or on *top* of it, lies in one word -

obedience. Do what He prompts you to do, and immediately you'll begin to feel better!

7

SET UP FOR A BLESSING

You say, "Would God talk to somebody like me?" Yes. Jesus said, "Henceforth I call you not servants; for the servant knoweth not what his Lord doeth: but I have called you friends; for all things that I have heard of my Father I had made known unto you" (Jn 15:15).

The difference between a friend and a servant lies in what they *know*. Here Jesus was telling his disciples, "I'm bringing you from the place of obedience to the place of intimacy; from functioning without insight, to knowing My mind and My purposes. I had to see if you could ... take bad news and still keep a good attitude ... trust Me and not try to manipulate things ... follow My plan even when you couldn't see the big picture ... and you did, so now I no longer call you servants, but friends."

Before God destroyed Sodom and Gomorrah He discussed it with Abraham, because Abraham was called "the friend of God." Before He gave Israel His law He talked it over with Moses. Listen, "And the Lord spake unto Moses face to face, as a man speaketh unto his friend" (Ex 33:11). You ask, "Is such a relationship possible today?" Yes, but check the price tag!

David said, "The secret of the Lord is with them that fear him" (Ps 25:14). God will share things with His friends that He *won't* share with others. When you see somebody who's clear-headed in the midst of confusion and cool when the heat is on, it could just be, that they know a secret - one shared with them by a friend!

Realize that when God tells you to do certain things, He's not trying to make your life hard or put you in a straightjacket. *No, He's just setting you up for a blessing!* Listen, "Oh that ... they would fear me and keep all my commandments ... that it might go well with them" (Dt 5:29 NIV). On the other end of anything God asks you to do, you'll hear the words, "that it might go well with you."

Living in peace, instead of always "going to pieces," is easier once you learn to respond to God *immediately*. Don't hesitate. Don't negotiate. Don't rationalize. And whatever you do - don't run! For the only thing that's worse than running from obedience, is running smack-dab into the consequences of disobedience. Ask Jonah.

The prophet Samuel said, "To obey is better than sacrifice" (1Sa 15:22). Sometimes you'll have to sacrifice certain things in order to obey God. But it's better to do that than to ignore His promptings, forfeit His blessings, and live stressed-out.

God will sometimes require things of you that: (a) He doesn't seem to require of others; (b) He won't explain, and you can't understand; (c) when you've obeyed, you won't immediately see the benefits.

But if you're convinced that He has a unique plan for your life and that He loves you unconditionally, you'll abandon yourself to Him in trust, knowing that in the end it will "go well with you."

8

God Has It All Figured Out

God's plan for your life is set. It can't be changed anymore than His character can be changed.

You say, "But what about the sin of Adam and Eve - was *that* His plan too?" No. Satan created a dilemma when Adam sinned. He took what God loved and reduced it to doing what God hated. The idea was to hand God a problem He couldn't solve. For God to kill what He hated - sin - He'd have to destroy what He loved - man.

But God had a strategy in place long before Satan ever created the dilemma. Jesus was "... the Lamb slain from the foundation of the world" (Rev 13:8). Before there was a sinner on earth there was a Savior in heaven. That means there's *nothing* the devil can throw at you, that will thwart the plan and purpose of God for your life. Nothing!

God acts - He doesn't react. He's never on the

defensive - He's always on the offensive. He's not improvising as He goes along. His plan for your life is in place, He knows *precisely* what you need at every point along the way.

Think of it this way; the script is already written before you, the actor, arrive on stage. All you have to do is play the role He assigns you, and follow His direction. "You mean I've no choice?" you ask? Yes - submit and be blessed, or disobey and be sorry. That's it!

But there's something else I need to point out here.

Sometimes God *permits* things; other times He actually *plans* them! Either way, He's got your best interest at heart. Listen, "He performeth the thing that is appointed for me" (Job 23:14). When you hear words like "He has appointed it for me," it changes your perspective.

It's like flying. On the ground your view is limited, but from 10,000 feet up, everything looks different. Now you're seeing "the big picture!"

The Bible says that after Job came through his trials, he had twice as much as he started with (Job 42:10). Does that mean that if you lose a $30,000 a-year job you'll get back a $60,000 a-year one? Or that your checkbook will always balance, or your car never break down, or your health never come under attack? Hardly!

Sometimes God rewards your faith with things you *can't* measure in monetary value. Things like … character … peace you didn't have before … a fresh sense of purpose … protection from danger … favor with others … clearer understanding … more compassion … and new direction. What value would you place on *those*?

There are three things you need to keep in mind at all times:

1. God loves you, and He's in control of everything that concerns you (Ps 138:8).

2. As long as *you* can do it, He won't do it for you (Ecc 9:10).

3. In order to bless you, He'll sometimes move

in ways that are hard to understand (Ps 25:4). Why? So that when the answer comes, there'll be no doubt about *who* gets the credit!

9

MAKING DECISIONS

Are you trying to make an important decision about your future? If so, here are some guidelines to help you.

1. Don't ask God to bless your plans; ask Him to show you His - they're already blessed. And while we're on this point, remember, God will never tell you to do anything that doesn't line up with what He's already told you in His Word (Isa 8:20).

2. Make sure your goal is to glorify Him. This can be difficult, because the worst forms of pride, often masquerade behind feigned humility. The human body is amazing - just pat a man on the back, and his head begins to swell! (Jas 4:6).

3. Use your brain. God's guidance transcends human reasoning, but it doesn't exclude it. When God redeems you, He doesn't *remove* your mind, He *renews* it. So pray, then put it to work. (Ro 12:2).

4. Seasons aren't meant to be ignored. If it isn't God's timing - wait! In the right season the plan will be clear, the people you need will show up, and the funds will be provided. (Ecc 3:1).

5. Seek worthy counsel. Beware of those who patronize you for selfish reasons, but always listen to those who value what you value, and have been where you need to go. (Pr 27:17).

6. Never act without the facts, but never limit God to them. When knowledge won't take you another step, faith will carry you through, for *that's* what connects you to the power of God.

Jesus said, "Ask and it will be given to you; seek and you will find; knock and the door will be opened to you. For everyone who asks receives; and he who seeks finds; and to him who knocks the door will be opened" (Mt 7:7-8 NIV).

When I'm making an important decision and I need God's help, I use *"The Triple-A Strategy."* Ask. Answer. Act.

Knowing the right question to ask, is sometimes half the battle. The only stupid questions are the ones we *don't* ask because of pride or ignorance.

Sometimes finding the right answer means sorting through the chafe of other people's misinformation, in order to get to the right decision. But if you keep forging ahead, you'll begin to see a clearer picture emerging - one that lines up with your calling and your God-given goals.

Don't be over-eager. Refuse to make choices based on your *present* perspective, rather than the *big picture* that will emerge if you just keep seeking.

Once you've asked, and answered all the questions you can, however, it's time to act. You can't let fear force you to linger in the shadows, waiting for a spotlight from heaven to provide you with assurance. When it's time to act - act!

Faith is like stepping out on tissue paper, believing that when you do, God will put solid rock beneath your feet. After all, He said, "I am the Lord ... who teaches you what is best for you, who directs you in the way you should go" (Isa 48:17 NIV).

Are you trying to find the will of God concerning a particular situation? If so, you need to understand that He speaks to us in the following ways:

First, through proven leadership. Listen, "Obey them that have the rule over you, and submit yourselves" (Heb 13:17). Who speaks into your life? To whom are you submitted? When it comes to God's leading, I believe 5 percent comes by direct revelation, the other 95 percent through relationships.

Second, through your gifts. Listen, "A man's gift makes room for him" (Pr 18:16 NAS). When God is leading you, you won't need to kick the door open or force your way in. Your gift will bring a solution or meet a need; therefore, you'll be welcomed and valued.

Third, through your thoughts. Listen, we have the mind of Christ. (Ro 12:2). Imagine: when our minds have been renewed and lined up with His Word, God actually *thinks* through us.

Fourth, through open doors. Paul said, "For a great door and effectual is opened unto me, and there are many adversaries" (1Co 16:9). God will open the door for you; but you need to remember that when He does, every opportunity He gives you, will bring challenges too. That's what builds your faith and strengthens you for the future.

Fifth, through sanctified desires. David said, "Delight thyself also in the Lord; and he shall give thee the desires of thine heart" (Ps 37:4). Most of us have so abused our capacity for desire that we're afraid to trust it anymore. Don't be. When Jesus becomes the center of your affections, His desires automatically *become* your desires.

Sixth, through "a word" of confirmation. Listen, "And thine ears shall hear a word behind thee, saying, This is the way" (Isa 30:21). Please notice that this word only comes *after* you obey what God has told you to do! It's a word *behind* you, letting you know you've made the right decision and that you're on the right track.

You *can* be led by God! Let that sink in! Listen, "The Lord watches over all the plans and paths of godly men" (Ps 1:6 LB). That includes you!

10

WHEN DOORS ARE CLOSED

The contract on your dream home just fell through. The promotion you were so sure of fizzled out at the last minute. The one person you *knew* would fulfill all your dreams, suddenly walked away. Slam! Slam! Slam! Doors you thought God had opened, suddenly become curtains of steel. Now you're asking, "Where's God in all of this? What's He doing anyway? Why has He placed me in this dead-end street?"

Despite your disappointment remember this - God is *still* directing your steps. Listen, "The steps of a good man are ordered by the Lord" (Ps 37:23). My friend, Sarah Utterbach, says, "My *steps*, and my *stops*, are ordered by the Lord." Think about that.

But, you say, "That house was just perfect … I really needed the money from that promotion … there's nobody else I want." From your limited perspective that may seem true, but understand, God alone can see into the future!

When your hopes have been crushed and doors have slammed in your face, rely on His wisdom and unfailing love. He has *already* planned your end from your beginning. (Isa 46:10-11). Trust Him to work it out for you. Give it a little more time and your pain will turn to praise as you realize that He simply closed a lesser door, to open a greater one.

Timing is so important! When you begin to understand God's timing, you'll be able to cooperate better with His plan for your life. When you don't know, learn to wait with confidence on the One who does.

The problem most of us have is, we attempt to take *the lead role* in our relationship with Him, and it doesn't work. He has that role, and He won't give it to us. He gives the instructions, and we follow - even though we don't always like or understand the way He takes us.

"Why does God take so long to do things?" you ask. *Because trust requires unanswered questions! When you don't know, you have to trust the One who does, and that keeps you growing in faith!*

God has a plan and a time, and while He's getting us ready He keeps us - *in His waiting room!* If that's where you are today, remember, it's only as you reach new levels of *maturity* that He releases new levels of *blessing* into your life.

11

THE REASON FOR THE STRUGGLE

One day a man found the cocoon of an emperor moth and took it home so that he could observe it coming out. Gradually a small opening appeared, and he watched as the moth struggled to force its body through. This went on for hours, then suddenly it stopped making progress. It seemed to have gotten as far as it could go. Thinking he would help, the man took scissors and made the opening wider, and the moth emerged easily. But when it did, he noticed that it had a swollen body, shriveled wings, and couldn't fly.

In that moment he realized that it was the *struggle* that caused its wings to form and its body to develop. *Freedom and flight could not come any other way!*

Are you struggling today? Are you wondering, "Why am I going through this?" Listen, "Let endurance and steadfastness and patience [notice those three qualities carefully] have full play and do a thorough work, so that you may be ... fully developed" (Jas 1:4 AMP).

God is more interested in your character than He is in your comfort. Overcoming obstacles is what develops in you the qualities needed to fulfill His purpose for your life. *The truth is, it can't happen any other way.*

In 2 Corinthians, Chapter 1, Paul spells out for us the benefits of going through hard times. Yes, there are actually *benefits*. Let's take a moment and look at them.

1. *"So that we may be able to comfort those who are in any affliction"* (2Co 1:4 NAS). My friend, Mike Murdock, says, "Only the broken become masters at mending." He's right! Built into any problem that forces you to grow, is the medicine that will make others whole. When you can say, "I've been there," people listen. Experience is one of your greatest assets - use it.

2. *"That we should not trust in ourselves"* (2Co 1:9 NAS). Anything that causes you to turn to God and lean harder on Him, is a blessing. Yet so often it's only when we lose a marriage, a loved one, our health, or our peace of mind, that we turn to Him.

3. *"That thanks may be given"* (2Co 1:11 NAS). Do you remember what your life was like before you met the Lord? David said, "Oh that men would praise the Lord for his goodness" (Ps 107:8). You need to stop today, lift up your heart, and begin to praise Him for all He has done for you. After all, where would you be without Him? *It doesn't bear thinking about - does it?*

12

OVERCOMING FEAR

"Jezebel ... sent this message to Elijah; 'You killed my prophets, and now ... I am going to kill you' ... so Elijah fled for his life" (1Ki 19:1-3LB).

The voice of Jezebel drove Elijah into a cave. The still small voice of God brought him back out. That's the key - if only you can hear the voice of God, you can face anything and overcome it.

So often the voice of Jezebel comes *after* you've had a mountain-top experience. Imagine, Elijah had just called down fire from heaven and been publicly honored. Then Jezebel sent word saying, "I'm going to kill you." She didn't use chariots and soldiers; she didn't need to - her *words* intimidated him, depressed him, robbed him of victory, and drove him into hiding.

Look out - the words the enemy uses will often come from *someone close to you* or even out of your *own* mouth!

The voice of Jezebel can cause you to fear cancer. "Your mother got it, so you'll get it too." Now you can't even take a shower without checking for lumps! The voice of Jezebel can cause you to fear financial ruin. "You'll lose your job - they'll foreclose on the house - you'll find yourself out on the street."

If you listen to that voice, you'll be afraid of the next telephone call, the next letter, or the next board meeting. Whose report are you going to believe? Who are you going to listen to?

The answer is - neither the wind, nor the fire, nor the earthquake could bring Elijah out of that cave. Only the still small voice of God could do that!

Dr. E.V. Hill tells the story of a lad taking a short cut home late one night through a vacant lot. It was very dark and the tall buildings cast ominous shadows all around him. Suddenly he became aware of someone following him. The faster he walked, the faster they walked. Frightened and frustrated, he finally turned to see who was following him, but when he did, there was no one there. Turning to continue home, he heard the noise again.

That's when he realized he was just hearing the legs of his corduroy pants rubbing together!

You may smile, but often our fear is just the result of two things:

1. Imagination. It will cause you to fear the worst, if you don't keep it under control (2Co 10:5).

2. Misunderstanding. Listen, "Fear brings with it the thought of punishment" (1Jn 4:18 AMP). Did you get that? When something goes wrong, we wonder, "Is God punishing me for something I've done?" The answer is, "Probably not." Fear and faith will be present with us every day; *the one we choose will rule our lives!*

When you come up against a fear-producing situation, immediately do the following: (a) Pray for God's wisdom and protection. He guarantees it. (b) Admit your inner struggle. You're not unique;

we all battle fear. (c) Stand on His promises, for He says, "I will never leave you nor forsake you" (Heb 13:5).

If you're battling fear today, listen to these words from the God who loves you beyond expression, protects you around the clock, and goes with you wherever you go.

When there seems to be no way out, He says to you, "Fear not; stand still [firm, confident, undismayed] and see the salvation of the Lord which He will work for you today" (Ex 14:13 AMP). Notice the words "… He will work for you today." Start looking for evidence of His hand at work in your situation. That's how your faith grows.

When the problem looks too big, He says to you, "Be strong, courageous, and firm; fear not nor be in terror before them, for it is the Lord your God who goes with you; he will not fail you or forsake you" (Dt 31:6 AMP). Stop and remind yourself whose company you're in. When I was a child, anytime I couldn't handle the fight I was in, I just called for my big brother, Neil.

When you feel like you just can't cope anymore, He says to you, "Do not look around you in terror and be dismayed, for I am your God. I will strengthen and harden you to difficulties. (Isa 41:10 AMP). Notice the words "... harden you to difficulties." God doesn't always lift us out of the problem, He takes us through it, in order to toughen us up.

When you lose your peace of mind, He says to you, "Do not fret or have anxiety about anything, but in every circumstance ... continue to make your wants known to God. And God's peace ... which transcends all understanding, shall garrison and mount guard over your hearts and minds" (Php 4:6-7 AMP).

What more could you ask for?

13

WALTER AND ARTHUR

Here's one of my favorite stories on *guidance*.

One day Walter drove his friend Arthur out into the country to see a piece of land with a couple of old shacks on it. When they arrived, Walter began describing the incredible things he was going to build there. He wanted his friend to buy some of the surrounding acreage, so he explained to him that in the next five years, the value of this land was going to increase several hundred times.

Although he never said it, Arthur thought, "Who in the world is going to drive 25 miles out into the middle of nowhere to see some crazy project? He's lost his mind!" So he mumbled something about being in a tight money situation and promised to look into it later. "Later will be too late," said Walter. "You'd better move now."

But Arthur couldn't see it.

And so it was, that Art Linkletter turned down an opportunity to buy the acreage that now surrounds Disneyland - the land his friend, Walt Disney, tried to persuade him to buy!

Every day opportunities are coming toward you - or passing you right by. The key is having the discernment to recognize them and the courage to step out and act on them.

God has … ideas … insights … and introductions … He longs to share with you. Any one of them could change your life forever. That's why He says, "I am the Lord your God, who *teaches* you what is best for you, who *directs* you in the way you should go" (Isa 48:17 NIV).

14

THE FAVOR OF GOD

"**I** will give this people favor in the sight of the Egyptians: and … when you go, ye shall not go empty" (Ex 3:31). God said He'd give His people *two* things before they left Egypt: favor with their enemies and great blessings. When He brought them out - they had both!

There's a lesson here for you!

Your present trouble is only a classroom - a controlled environment for God to work on your behalf. Look what He used to free His people from slavery and turn their situation around - flies, hailstones, and frogs. What a committee! There's *nothing* He can't do. He can be your doctor, your counselor, your broker, your lawyer, and anything else you need Him to be.

Notice; the frogs that invaded the homes of the Egyptians, couldn't cross the property line of

God's people. Why? *Because the favor of God will protect you!* Think of the things that have come right up to you, but didn't touch you. That's because God's Word says, "Neither shall any plague come nigh thy dwelling" (Ps 91:10).

The same Pharaoh, who had repeatedly said "no" to Moses, suddenly said "yes." How come? Timing! When the time is right, God will move on your behalf! So start expecting favor; favor from unexpected places; favor that moves mountains; favor that opens doors; favor that gives you access to things you otherwise wouldn't have.

If you can't cope with the future, check with the past. Listen, "Surely [not maybe] goodness and mercy *shall* follow me all the days of my life ..." (Ps 23:6). Are you facing a situation today that you don't know how to handle? Are you getting conflicting opinions and advice? Is the decision you have to make so important that you're afraid to make it, in case you make the wrong call? If so, you're in the right place for God to speak to you.

Here's a prayer for you today:

Lord, Your Word says You are "the only wise God," and I am desperately in need of You at this time. I find myself in a situation that human wisdom can't explain, and human ability can't fix. There's only one way out - that's through it!

Send the Spirit of Wisdom to show me how to walk wisely. Send the Spirit of Revelation to help me understand what I can't figure out, for Your understanding alone will get me through this.

Help me to faithfully do all that You show me to do, and to remember that the wisdom of this world is foolishness to You. Help me to know the difference between human advice and godly advice, and always to choose Your way.

I submit this situation to You now and commit myself to following You, knowing that You have promised to direct my steps. In Christ's Name. AMEN.

15

Special Prayers

In the following pages you'll find prayers you can use when you're not sure how to approach God, or what to do! Each one is based on the *promises* of His Word, so you can pray them with confidence and *expect* results.

When You Need To Recommit Your Life to God

"Let the wicked forsake his way, and the unrighteous man his thoughts: and let him return unto the Lord, and he will have mercy upon him; and to our God, for he will abundantly pardon." Isaiah 55:7

Father, forgive me for taking back control of my life and living as if You didn't exist.

If there was a way I could *earn* Your acceptance, I would do it, but Your Word tells me that the only sacrifice You want is a broken spirit (Ps 51:17). So today I come before You, surrendering, repenting, and asking You to cleanse me, renew me, and fill me with Your Spirit once again.

Thank You for remaining faithful to me, even though I was unfaithful to You. Thank You for loving me when I didn't love You in return; for drawing me back, even when I tried to ignore the conviction of Your Holy Spirit.

I renounce my selfish ways and choose to follow You, making You Lord of my life!

I commit myself to developing relationships with those who love You, to spending time in prayer and in Your Word, to remaining loyal to Your house where I can receive from You, and in turn, give to others, out of what You have given to me.

You said that You would rather I was hot or cold, but not luke warm. Light a fire in me today that will burn so brightly, that others will be drawn to You. In Christ's name. AMEN.

WHEN IT'S HARD TO WAIT

"So do not throw away your confidence; it will be richly rewarded. You need to persevere so that when you have done the will of God, you will receive what he has promised." Hebrews 10:35-36 NIV

God, I've done everything I know to see my dreams come true. I've had seasons of working hard and seasons "of letting go and letting God." Still, the things I've believed for, seem like they'll never happen.

Like Sarah - I feel as if I'll never hold the one thing I long for most. God, don't let me miss my destiny. Don't let me hope for things that are not part of Your plan for my life. Let me hear Your voice, reassuring me that I'm believing according to Your will.

Remind me again of Your promises to me, so that my faith will be strengthened, and I can take hold of them. Help me to understand the difference between what I must go after and what I must wait on You for.

When it's up to *me*, give me the strength to demolish doubt and march fearlessly into the new day You've prepared for me. When it's up to *You*, give me the grace and patience to wait; fill me with the joyful anticipation that accompanies a perfectly timed present.

Lord, they say that You are never, ever late. In these days of waiting, when time seems endless, keep me strong in faith. Don't let me stop short of my blessing. Remind me again that I must not throw away my confidence for it will be richly rewarded! In Christ's name. AMEN.

WHEN YOU'VE LOST A CHILD

"Even when I walk through the dark valley of death, I will not be afraid, for you are close beside me."

Psalm 23:4 NLT

Lord, I cannot imagine any grief more consuming than this.

O God, my child. I am weary and numb. It is hard for me to realize that this loss is real and that it is permanent.

I feel guilty that, as a parent, it is so hard to release my child to You, the Father. But Lord, it is almost more than I can bear.

Come and bring comfort. Send Your Holy Spirit in a way I've never experienced before. I need You right beside me. I need to cry on Your shoulder. I need to know that You know, You really know.

Lord, give wisdom to those around me who want to help but feel so inadequate. Equip them to minister to me in ways that will help all of us.

But more than that, be my deepest friend. Bring me through these devastating days. Give me grace through all my grief.

Help me now to survive, and when it's time, to arise stronger and more compassionate. Remind me that my child is safe with You. And so am I. In Christ's name. AMEN.

WHEN YOU'VE BEEN PHYSICALLY OR EMOTIONALLY ABUSED

"The angel of the Lord encamps around those who fear him, and he delivers them."   Psalm 34:7 NIV

Father, I feel such a sense of shame and despair. Today, I'm desperately in need of You. Put a hedge of protection around me and my family. Shield us from further harm, for You promised You would bless the righteous with favor; and surround them like a shield (Ps 5:12 NKJV).

Your Word says that whatever I bind on earth, You will bind in heaven, and whatever I loose on earth, You will loose in heaven (Mt 16:19). Today, I bind the spirit of anger and violence over this family and loose the Spirit of peace and self-control, especially in my spouse.

The enemy has tried repeatedly to tell me it's all my fault. But I refuse to accept the blame for somebody else's behavior, or to allow it to take root in my family. Stop this generational sin now!

Prevent us from "acting out" in the future, what we have experienced in the past.

Bring repentance and restoration to this relationship and keep us safe while you're doing it. Your Word says, "You are my hiding place; you will preserve me from trouble" (Ps 32:7 NKJV). I claim that promise now!

In this time of fear and confusion, give me the strength to continue, the courage to confide in someone worthy of my trust, and, if necessary, the wisdom to know when and how to leave. In Christ's name. AMEN.

WHEN IT'S TIME TO MOVE

"And the Lord, he it is that doth go before thee: he will be with thee, he will not fail thee, neither forsake thee: fear not, neither be dismayed."

Deuteronomy 31:8

Father, since You've promised to go before me, I move forward with confidence, knowing that Your plans for me include prosperity, safety, hope, and a future of blessing (Jer 29:11).

I choose to see this move as an opportunity to start over, leaving behind the defeats and negative habits of the past; to begin adding to my faith, goodness, knowledge, self-control, perseverance, godliness, brotherly kindness, and love in increasing measure (2Pe 1:5-8).

Lead me into relationships with those who add to me, not subtract from me; who challenge me to reach higher and grow deeper in my walk with You.

Help my children to adjust. Bring into their

lives the right friends; ones that build them up, not tear them down. Use this move to mature them and teach them to rely more on You.

Good Shepherd, lead me, guide me, and protect me. Send reminders along the way that You are with me and that my best days are yet to be. In Christ's name. Amen.

WHEN NO ONE UNDERSTANDS

"But he knoweth the way that I take: when he hath tried me, I shall come forth as gold."   Job 23:10

God, I feel like there's not a living soul who understands me at the moment. It's not that they don't want to understand, it's just that they *can't*.

You've given me gifts and an assignment, they don't seem to comprehend, and you've given them gifts and a path to walk, that are equally puzzling to me. I know this is how Your body works, and by faith I accept it, yet there's a loneliness in me that surpasses anything I've ever known.

But as frustrated as I am at the moment, I still say 'Yes' to you Lord, because all Your ways are perfect, and nobody knows better than You, how it feels to be misunderstood.

Help me to walk this road with confidence in You; with the courage that comes from knowing I am Yours. Help me to cling to my convictions, yet still love those who misunderstand me.

Keep me far from anger and close to Your heart, and though it's an up-hill climb, take my hand, light my way, and help me to walk on, for in the end I know that *all* things will work together for my good and Your glory. In Christ's name. AMEN.

When You're Searching for the Right Job

"Trust in the Lord with all your heart and lean not on your own understanding. In all your ways acknowledge him, and he shall direct your paths."

Proverbs 3:5-6 NKJV

Heavenly Father, give me an unmistakable sense of Your direction. Open the doors that *You* have ordained, and close those that don't fit into Your plan for my life.

Regardless of how enticing an offer may be, teach me to lean on *your* understanding, not mine, for more important to me than income or benefits, is being in the center of Your will.

Your Word declares that You delight in seeing me prosper (Ps 35:27). Your promise is that in all things, at all times, having all I need, I will abound in every good work (2Co 9:8 NIV). I claim those promises!

Give me an assignment that lines up with my

gifts and Your purposes; one that operates as both a source of abundance and as an outlet for ministry to others.

Today, I commit myself to walk in faith and patience, and not jump into something out of desperation or fear.

Help me to know the difference between what's good and what's best, and to wait only for the best, for that's what You desire for me. In Christ's name. AMEN.

When It's Hard To Surrender to God

"Therefore, I urge you, brothers, in view of God's mercy, to offer your bodies as living sacrifices, holy and pleasing to God." Romans 12:1 NIV

Lord, there's only one way to have *more* of You, and that's to have *less* of me. Help me today, for "dying to myself" is the hardest thing I've ever done.

I *want* to sacrifice, but I keep discovering how much I'm holding on to my life, my hopes, my dreams - my stuff.

Lead me to the place where I can gladly let go; where I can release everything and offer it to You.

I want to give You more than I have and more than I am. I want to learn to give what I'd rather keep; not out of law, but out of love.

Give me more love, so that I can love You more. Give me more gratitude, so that I can be more grateful than I am.

Today, I lay myself on Your altar. You know

this heart so well - its flaws, its frailty, its fire. Send Your fire and purify me. Make me completely Yours; a living sacrifice, pleasing and acceptable to You. In Christ's name. AMEN.

Bob's *Newest* Book

AUTHOR BOB GASS

Joy

COMES IN THE MORNING

Finding Comfort in the Time of Loss

At some point we all lose what we love…this insightful book will show you how to deal with loss and turn your grief into a healing force.

If you know someone dealing with grief, this book is a very special gift to help them through their difficult time.

To order this, and more great books by the author, please order online at our website: www.bobgass.com or call 1-800-964-9846.

Hardcover

GOD STILL HEALS TODAY

Insights from Bob Gass

you can be HEALED
GOD STILL HEALS TODAY
By Bob Gass

Bob addresses
these questions:

Is it God's will to heal?

*Why are some
not healed?*

*How to maintain
your healing.*

*The importance of
knowing God's Word.*

Visit our web site at
www.bobgass.com
for other great books
by the author.

Paperback

HOW TO LIVE
Worry Free!

Bob Gass

Be Not Afraid

HOW TO CONQUER YOUR FEARS

Bob Gass

Hardcover

Fear distorts our view of life! It tells us we're not safe in God's hands; that He's not big enough to take care of us.

The question is, *"How will you ever know, unless you push beyond the fear and experience the abundant life Jesus promised you?"*

In this book, Bob Gass tells you how to conquer your **financial** fears, **family** fears, fear of **sickness,** and even fear of **death.** This book will change your life!

VISIT OUR WEB SITE AT
www.bobgass.com